COBBLERS, CRUMBLES & CRISPS
AND OTHER OLD-FASHIONED FRUIT DESSERTS

COBBLERS, CRUMBLES & CRISPS

AND OTHER OLD-FASHIONED FRUIT DESSERTS

LINDA ZIMMERMAN AND PEGGY MELLODY

Illustrations by Sally Sturman

Clarkson Potter/Publishers
New York

Published by Clarkson N. Potter, Inc.,
201 East 50th Street, New York, New York 10022.
Member of the Crown Publishing Group.

CLARKSON N. POTTER, POTTER and colophon are trademarks of
Clarkson N. Potter, Inc.

Manufactured in the United States of America

Library of Congress Cataloging in Publication Data
Zimmerman, Linda.
Cobblers, crumbles, and crisps and other old-fashioned fruit desserts/
by Linda Zimmerman and Peggy Mellody.
p.   cm.
Includes index.
1. Desserts.   2. Cookery (Fruit)   I. Mellody, Peggy.   II. Title.
TX773.Z547   1991
641.8'6—dc20   90-48898
CIP

ISBN 0-517-57489-6

Design by Barbara B. Kantor

10   9   8   7   6   5

CONTENTS

TO OUR MOTHERS—
JEAN ZIMMERMAN AND NANCY MELLODY

INTRODUCTION

Old-fashioned fruit desserts evoke images of huge country kitchens and the food our grandmothers fed us when we were kids. Like most traditional dishes in this country, these desserts had their beginnings as adaptations of familiar Old World recipes using available American regional ingredients. For some unknown reason, many of these recipes go by two or three different names, depending upon their area of origination. But whether from early New England, our Midwest farm country, the deep South, or the Old West, cobblers, buckles, betties, pandowdies, crisps, crumbles, deep-dish pies, and even fruit compotes are an integral part of our American culinary tradition.

We've tried to demystify these desserts by providing definitions that apply to how they are prepared or served today.

COBBLERS are similar to deep-dish pies and topped with a sweet pastry or biscuit-type crust. The fruit is lightly sweetened, tossed with a small amount of thickener if particularly juicy, topped with crust that is sprinkled with sugar, then baked. John Mariani in his *Dictionary of American Food and Drink* (Ticknor & Fields, 1983) claims that "a cobbler is a western deep-dish pie with a thick crust and a fruit filling," served with toppings that vary depending on the area. According to Southern food authority Nathalie Dupree, a true cobbler starts with a clafoutis-type batter spread on the bottom of a buttered pan, then topped with the sweetened fruit and baked.

One theory regarding the name refers to the phrase "cobble up," meaning to put something together in a hurry. There is also the possibility that the name refers to the look of the finished dessert. The topping was probably made by dropping large dollops of biscuit or scone dough over the fruit, thus creating a cobblestone effect when baked. Now, pie dough or other pastry is sometimes substituted for the biscuit dough. The topping can be either a single sheet of pastry or sugar cookie dough, a lattice-style crust, or individual biscuits or scones whose degree of density depends only upon personal taste. Cobblers can also have both a top and a bottom crust.

PANDOWDY, similar to a deep-dish fruit pie, first was served on New England farms as a breakfast dish. It was made with apples, seasoned with butter, spices, and brown sugar or molasses, topped with a biscuit or pie crust, then baked and served warm with milk or cream. The name refers to the last step of the recipe when the crust, after a short baking time, is broken into pieces (referred to as "dowdying"), pushed down into the fruit, and the dish returned to the oven to finish baking.

SLUMPS AND GRUNTS also seem to have come from colonial America. Both are a type of stove-top cobbler consisting of stewed fruit and feathery-light steamed dumplings that absorb the cooking fruit juices. Grunts usually are made by stewing blueberries (or mixed berries) in a cast-iron skillet. Slumps are prepared with any type of fruit in either a saucepan or a skillet.

No one really knows how these names originated. Grunt is thought to refer to the sound made by the bubbling fruit when it was prepared in a kettle hanging over an open fire in the early days of America. Apple Slump was immortalized by Louisa May Alcott, author of *Little Women,* who called her home in Concord, Massachusetts, by that name.

CRUMBLES AND CRISPS in this book are interchangeable, since both are made with lightly sweetened fruit topped with an easily-put-together crumbly shortbread pastry. Crisps are called crumbles in Great Britain, where the toppings often contain rolled oats in addition to flour.

BETTYS were also a colonial favorite, and are a cousin to crisps and crumbles. Originally they were made of layers of sweetened and spiced apples and buttered crumbs. Today, layers of bread cubes often replace the crumbs, and any fruit can be substituted for the apples.

BAKED DUMPLINGS pertain to either pastries filled with a fruit mixture or whole fruits wrapped in a flaky dough, then baked until the fruit is soft and the pastry light golden.

STEAMED DUMPLINGS are made by dropping dollops of dough or batter on top of the cooking fruit. The dumplings are steamed until cooked through and lightly saturated with the fruit juices. Innumerable recipes for boiled fruit dumplings can be found in Early American cookbooks. Wrapped in cloth, they were immersed in boiling water, cooked until the fruit was soft, and usually served hot with custard sauce.

PIES is a generic term for dishes made with crust and filling. The fruit is usually cooked, sometimes lightly thickened, and always sweetened before being poured into the shell.

TARTS are usually prebaked single-crust pastry shells filled with a thin layer of custard or pastry cream and topped with fresh fruit. Sometimes they're finished with a sweet glaze. Small handpies are also called tarts.

SHORTCAKES are crumbly biscuits enriched with sweet butter or cream and eggs sandwiched with fruit and soft whipped cream.

BUCKLES are similar to coffee or breakfast cakes, and were traditionally made with berries folded into or strewn over the batter before baking. They are cut into squares before serving.

FRITTERS are made by dipping sliced fruit into a thick, sweetened batter and deep-frying in unflavored oil. They can also be prepared like pancakes by stirring small chunks of fruit into the batter and spooning onto a lightly oiled hot skillet.

FOOLS, which originated in England, are delicious fruit creams, consisting of sweetened, pureed, stewed, or uncooked fruits folded into an equal amount of lightly whipped cream.

FLUMMERIES are thickened fruit puddings, usually made with berries, that are highly favored in New England where wild blueberries are found. Cornstarch is the preferred thickener in the United States, but in Europe, oatmeal and other cereal grains are used, creating a much tastier and more substantial dessert.

All of these wonderful desserts can be found in the following pages. For your convenience, recipes using similar ingredients and preparation techniques have been grouped together in each of five chapters.

"Cobblers, Pandowdies, Slumps, and Grunts" is filled with variations of homey deep-dish standards that double as elegant company standouts. You'll find Brandied Apricot Cobbler, Peach Cobbler, the delicate pink Apple, Quince, and Dried Cherry Pandowdy, and a Boysenberry-Peach Slump with its surprisingly light lime-scented dumplings, delicious for a lazy Sunday brunch.

Most of the "Crumbles, Crisps, and Bettys" can be assembled in minutes, popped into the oven, and forgotten until serving time. Apple-Cheddar Crumble combines two favorite American flavors; After-School Date Crumbles, with their streusel-like topping, are old-fashioned bar cookies; and two unusual twists to old American standards are the Apple, Rhubarb, and Fennel Crisp, infused with toasted crushed fennel seeds, and the Autumn Harvest Brown Betty, smothered by an unusual crunchy and chewy buttered dry cereal topping.

"Dumplings, Pies, and Tarts" are all fruit-filled flaky pastries. Nectarine and Wild Blueberry Dumplings are a lovely dessert for a summer evening barbecue. Connie Bates's Cherry Pie, with its butter cookie–like crust, is one of the best cherry and pastry combinations we've ever tasted. And for a breakfast treat with a steaming cup of café au lait, try our Banberry Tarts, with plumped dried cranberries and golden raisins stuffed into a delicate cream cheese pastry.

"Shortcakes, Batter Cakes, and Buckles" includes Better-Than-Best Old-fashioned Strawberry Shortcake plus a selection of recipes with some new approaches to an old theme. Try the sophisticated Warm Rhubarb Shortcakes with Hot Butterscotch Sauce, an unusual combination of tart and sweet; Pineapple–Macadamia Nut Upside-down Cake with its heady sweet and spicy-hot marriage of fresh pineapple chunks and crystallized ginger; and Blueberry Gingerbread Buckle, which transforms an ordinary plain Jane dessert into a dazzling explosion of New England flavors.

In "Fritters, Fools, and Other Fruit Favorites" you'll find Papaya Fritters, the fruit wrapped in a delicate, sweet tempuralike batter that is equally delicious with any fruit of your choice. Baked Apples with Date-Nut Filling and Peppered Pears in Red Wine are easily prepared in advance, and the scrumptious "Hot" Banana Split à la Yanks is foolproof, barely taking any effort to put together.

There is also a chapter of "Master Recipes," which includes a variety of pastry crusts and several sauces and toppings, all of which can be referred to for any of your other baking.

INGREDIENTS AND TIPS
◆

All of our recipes can be prepared without any special kitchen equipment. Electric mixers and food processors speed up preparation, but because the recipes are so simple, they can just as easily be made by hand.

FRUIT. Unless otherwise called for, use fresh ripe fruit. We specify peeling such fruits as peaches, nectarines, and apricots, but if you prefer the skins left on, the dishes will be equally delicious. A 10-second dip in boiling water helps to slip off the skins if they're difficult to remove with a knife. Apples and pears are easily peeled with a potato peeler.

The amounts of fruit given are just guidelines. Since most of the recipes call for fruit that's piled high into baking dishes, it's a matter of taste or availability that determines the quantity used, and the spices and sugar should be adjusted to taste accordingly. The amount of sugar needed will also vary depending upon the sweetness provided by the fruit itself or your personal preference.

FLOUR. Any flours will work with crumble and crisp toppings. For the flakiest pie crusts and the lightest cakes, unless we have designated a specific type of flour, use unbleached or bleached white flour.

FATS. Unless shortening is specified, we prefer the taste of butter. Use unsalted butter or unsalted margarine or a butter-margarine blend. You cannot substitute whipped butter or light or diet margarine in these recipes because of the difference in volume and water content. No-stick vegetable oil sprays are a good way to cut calories when greasing your baking pans.

DAIRY PRODUCTS. If possible, avoid "ultrapasteurized" cream, which we find lends a bitter aftertaste. Health food stores and specialty markets are the best source of raw or pasteurized cream, sour cream, and cream cheese. Milk, half-and-half, and cream are interchangeable in our recipes. Just remember that a richer dessert is the result of the higher fat content.

EGGS. Unless specified, all our recipes are made with large eggs, which can be used straight from the refrigerator. When whipping egg whites, more volume is produced if the eggs are first brought to room temperature.

FLAVORED SUGARS. Mix 4 teaspoons of ground cinnamon into each 1 cup of granulated sugar. Store in a flour dredger or any spice jar with a sprinkle top. We also like to flavor our sugar with vanilla by burying a whole vanilla bean in a tightly sealed canister. Just replace the sugar as it is used. The vanilla bean will keep indefinitely.

PASTRY NOTES. The secret of light and flaky biscuits, short-cakes, and pie crusts is in the handling. Do not overmix the dough. A wire pastry blender, a large fork, two butter knives used scissors fashion, or your fingers all work equally well for rubbing butter into flour. A quick method is to use a food processor fitted with a steel blade. All liquids and fats should be ice cold.

COBBLERS,
PANDOWDIES, SLUMPS,
AND GRUNTS

◆

BRANDIED APRICOT COBBLER

◆

Any variety of apricot makes a superb cobbler.

SERVES 6

¾ cup plus I tablespoon sugar

I tablespoon cornstarch

¼ cup high-quality brandy

I tablespoon fresh lemon juice

½ teaspoon grated lemon zest

½ teaspoon ground nutmeg

2 pounds (about 18–20) ripe apricots, peeled or unpeeled, pitted and sliced (4 cups)

1½ cups cake flour

1½ teaspoons baking powder

¼ teaspoon salt

4 tablespoons (½ stick) cold unsalted butter, cut into pieces

2 large egg yolks

⅓ cup sour cream

Preheat the oven to 400° F.

Mix 3 tablespoons of the sugar, cornstarch, brandy, lemon juice, zest, and nutmeg in a 2- or 3-quart baking dish. Stir in the apricots and toss to evenly coat.

Put the flour, remaining sugar, baking powder, and salt into a large bowl; stir to mix well. Add the butter and cut in with a pastry blender or rub in with your fingers until the mixture looks like coarse crumbs.

Beat the yolks and sour cream with a fork to blend. Pour over the flour mixture and stir with a fork just until the dough is moistened. Drop spoonfuls of the batter over the apricots. Sprinkle the cobbler with the remaining sugar.

Bake for 30 to 35 minutes or until the topping is golden brown and the filling is bubbling. Let cool 10 minutes before serving.

PEACH COBBLER

◆

This cobbler was inspired by one we ate at L.A. Nicola, a small neighborhood restaurant in Los Angeles.

SERVES 4 TO 6

1	cup all-purpose flour
2	teaspoons baking powder
½	cup sugar
6	tablespoons cold unsalted butter, cut into pieces
1	large egg, lightly beaten
¼	cup half-and-half
2½	pounds fresh peaches, peeled, pitted, and cut into ¼-inch slices (5 to 6 cups)
2	tablespoons fresh lemon juice
2	tablespoons apricot preserves
1	teaspoon ground mace
½	teaspoon ground cinnamon mixed with 2 tablespoons sugar
	Vanilla ice cream

Preheat the oven to 350° F.

Put the flour, baking powder, and ¼ cup of the sugar in a large bowl. Stir to mix well. Add 4 tablespoons of the butter and cut in with a pastry blender or rub in with your fingers until the mixture resembles coarse crumbs. Beat the egg and half-and-half together in a measuring cup. Stir into the flour with a fork just until the dough is moistened. Shape the dough into a ball and refrigerate for 15 minutes.

In a medium bowl, toss together the peaches, lemon juice, preserves, mace, and the remaining sugar. Pour the peaches into a 1½-quart oval baking dish. Dot with the remaining butter.

Roll out the dough to fit the top of the dish. Place it on top of the peaches and crimp the pastry edges to the sides of the pan to seal. Cut a few vents in the dough with a sharp knife. Sprinkle generously with the cinnamon sugar.

Bake for 30 to 35 minutes or until the crust is light golden. Serve hot with ice cream.

VARIATION

◆

PEACH AND APRICOT PANDOWDY. Add 2 cups apricots, peeled and quartered. Proceed as above. Bake 25 minutes in a 2-quart baking dish, remove from the oven, and "dowdy" the crust by cutting into it and the peaches with a sharp knife, pushing the pieces of crust into the fruit. Bake an additional 15 minutes. If the pandowdy looks too dry, add some peach nectar or other fruit nectar during baking. Serve hot with ice cream or heavy cream.

SOUTHERN SOUR CHERRY
AND RASPBERRY COBBLER

◆

Fresh sour cherries are difficult to find since most of those grown in the United States are canned. But if you can obtain the fresh cherries (our favorites are Morellos), by all means use them, substituting an equal quantity and adjusting the sugar to taste.

SERVES 6 TO 8

2 teaspoons unsalted butter, softened
1 cup cake flour
1½ teaspoons baking powder
½ teaspoon salt
½ cup sugar
9 tablespoons unsalted butter, melted
½ cup milk
½ teaspoon vanilla extract
1 16-ounce can (about 2 cups) pitted
   sour cherries, drained
2 cups fresh raspberries or frozen
   unsweetened raspberries (about ½
   pound)
⅔ cup sugar
1 tablespoon quick tapioca
   Heavy cream or vanilla ice cream

Preheat the oven to 350° F.

Grease an 8-inch square baking pan with the 2 teaspoons of softened butter.

Combine the flour, baking powder, salt, and sugar in a medium bowl. Make a well. Add the melted butter, milk, and vanilla. Mix until blended. Pour the batter into the prepared pan.

In a clean bowl, combine the cherries, raspberries, sugar, and tapioca. Spoon the fruit mixture and any sauce evenly over the batter.

Bake for 35 to 40 minutes, or until the batter is golden and puffed around the fruit. Spoon into bowls and serve hot or warm with heavy cream or ice cream.

BRITISH ISLES
BLACKBERRY COBBLER

◆

In England, blackberries traditionally are paired with apples for this cobbler, but we use only the berries to show off their delectable flavor.

SERVES 6

1	recipe for Easy Cream Cheese Pastry (page 108), chilled
6	cups blackberries
1¼	cups plus 1 tablespoon sugar
¼	cup cornstarch
	Heavy cream or vanilla ice cream

Preheat the oven to 400° F.

Remove the pastry from the refrigerator and divide it into 6 pieces. On a lightly floured surface or between two pieces of wax paper, roll out each piece of dough to form a 4½- or 5-inch circle about ¼-inch thick.

Combine the blackberries, 1¼ cups of the sugar, and the cornstarch in a large bowl. Divide the filling among six 4-inch tartlet or potpie pans.

Place one circle of pastry on top of each pan, making sure the berries are completely covered. Crimp pastry edges to the sides of the pan to seal. Make 3 slits in the top of the pastry with a sharp knife. Sprinkle with remaining sugar.

Bake 35 to 45 minutes, or until the pastry is a light golden brown and the filling is bubbling. Serve warm topped with heavy cream or ice cream.

NOTE: If preparing these cobblers in advance for the freezer, don't slit the pastry until you're ready to bake. And make sure to use tart or potpie pans that can go directly from freezer to oven. Bake in a preheated 425° F. oven on the lowest shelf for 10 minutes, then reduce the temperature to 375° F. and proceed as above.

SPICED BLUEBERRY AND MAPLE CORNMEAL COBBLER

◆

The light corn bread and spiced fresh blueberries make a winning combination.

SERVES 6

4 cups (about 1½ pints) fresh blueberries

1 cup plus 2 tablespoons granulated sugar

1 tablespoon quick tapioca

2 teaspoons grated lemon zest

1 teaspoon ground cinnamon

½ teaspoon ground nutmeg

1 cup all-purpose flour

½ cup yellow cornmeal

2 teaspoons baking powder

½ teaspoon baking soda

½ teaspoon salt

½ cup (1 stick) plus 2 tablespoons unsalted butter

1 cup confectioners' sugar

1 large egg

¾ cup buttermilk

2   **tablespoons maple syrup**
      Sweetened whipped cream or
         vanilla ice cream

Preheat the oven to 375° F.

Combine the blueberries, granulated sugar, tapioca, zest, cinnamon, and nutmeg in a shallow 10-inch baking dish or cast-iron skillet.

Combine the flour, cornmeal, baking powder, soda, and salt in a mixing bowl. Cream ½ cup of the butter with the confectioners' sugar until light and fluffy. Beat in the egg and buttermilk. Stir in the dry/ ingredients. Pour the batter evenly over the berries.

Bake for 35 to 40 minutes, or until the mixture is bubbly and the corn bread springs back when lightly touched. Remove from the oven. Raise the oven to broil.

Melt the remaining butter, mix with the maple syrup, and brush on the corn bread. Run under the broiler about 1 minute or until the top of the cobbler is lightly glazed. Serve warm with sweetened whipped cream or ice cream.

VARIATION

◆

DOUBLE BLUEBERRY BLUE CORNMEAL COBBLER. Substitute blue cornmeal for the yellow cornmeal, add ¼ cup dried or fresh wild blueberries to the batter, proceed as above.

CINNAMON AND ORANGE
SCENTED PLUM PANDOWDY

◆

*A*ny type of plum is delicious.

SERVES 4 TO 6

1⅓	cups plus 3 tablespoons all-purpose flour
¼	cup fine white or yellow cornmeal
¼	teaspoon salt
2	tablespoons finely grated orange zest
¾	cup (1½ sticks) cold unsalted butter, cut into pieces
1	tablespoon fresh lemon juice
4 to 8	tablespoons ice water
2	pounds red plums, pitted and cut into eighths (6 cups, 12 medium)
½	cup firmly packed light brown sugar
¼	cup granulated sugar
¼	cup freshly squeezed orange juice
½	teaspoon ground nutmeg
	Pinch of ground cardamom
1 to 2	tablespoons milk
½	teaspoon ground cinnamon mixed with 2 tablespoons granulated sugar
	Heavy cream or vanilla ice cream

22

Put 1⅓ cups of the flour, the cornmeal, salt, and 1 tablespoon of the zest in a large bowl and mix well with a wooden spoon. Add 9 tablespoons of the butter and rub in with your fingers until the mixture resembles coarse crumbs.

With a large fork, stir in the lemon juice. Add the water one tablespoon at a time, just until the dough is firm, moist, and pliable. Roll into a ball and wrap in wax paper. Refrigerate 30 minutes.

Preheat the oven to 375° F.

Flatten the dough. On a lightly floured surface, roll it out to a ¼- to ⅛-inch thickness.

In a heavy medium saucepan combine the plums, sugars, remaining flour and zest, orange juice, nutmeg, and cardamom. Cook over medium heat, stirring occasionally until the mixture begins to thicken and boil, about 5 minutes. Boil 1 more minute and pour into a 1- or 1½-quart baking dish. Dot with the remaining butter.

Fit the pastry over the fruit, trimming the edges so the pastry just fits inside the dish. Brush with milk and sprinkle with the cinnamon sugar. With a sharp knife, cut a few vents in the dough.

Bake for 25 minutes or until light golden brown. Remove to a heatproof surface. "Dowdy" the crust by cutting down into it and the fruit with a sharp knife horizontally and vertically, cutting about 2-inch-size pieces. Push the crust into the fruit with the back of a spatula, allowing the fruit and juices to bubble up to the top. Bake an additional 15 minutes. Serve hot or warm with heavy cream or ice cream.

APPLE, QUINCE, AND DRIED CHERRY PANDOWDY

◆

Apple pandowdy, similar to deep-dish apple pie, originated as a New England farm breakfast dish served warm with milk or cream. In this recipe, the quince and dried cherries (available at specialty stores) add a lovely blush-pink hue to the apples.

SERVES 6

½ recipe for All-Purpose Fruit Pie
  Crust (page 110)

⅔ cup apple cider

2 tablespoons molasses

½ cup firmly packed dark brown sugar

3 tablespoons all-purpose flour

4 cups peeled and sliced tart green
  apples (3 to 5)

4 cups peeled and sliced quince (4 to 5)

½ cup dried cherries

2 teaspoons ground cinnamon

1 teaspoon finely grated fresh ginger,
  or 1 tablespoon finely chopped
  crystallized ginger

1 teaspoon ground nutmeg

¼ teaspoon ground cloves

5 tablespoons unsalted butter, cut into pieces
I to 2 tablespoons milk
½ teaspoon ground cinnamon mixed
 with 2 tablespoons granulated sugar
 Heavy cream or vanilla ice cream

Preheat the oven to 400° F.

Roll the pastry out on a lightly floured board to about ⅛-inch thickness.

In a large, heavy pot combine the cider, molasses, brown sugar, flour, apples, quince, cherries, spices, and 3 tablespoons of the butter. Cook over medium heat 10 to 15 minutes, stirring occasionally, until the fruit has softened. (Be careful that the fruit doesn't stick to the bottom of the pot.) Transfer to a 2-quart baking dish and dot with the remaining butter.

Fit the pastry over the top of the fruit, trimming the edges with a sharp knife so the pastry just fits inside the baking dish. Brush with milk and sprinkle with the cinnamon sugar. With the tip of a sharp knife, cut a few vents in the dough.

Bake 25 to 30 minutes or until light golden brown. Remove the dish from the oven to a heatproof surface. "Dowdy" the crust by cutting down into it and the fruit with a sharp knife horizontally and vertically, cutting about 2-inch-size pieces. Push the crust into the fruit with the back of a spatula, allowing the fruit and juices to bubble up to the top. Bake an additional 15 minutes. Spoon into bowls and serve hot or warm with heavy cream or ice cream.

BOYSENBERRY-PEACH SLUMP

◆

The boysenberry is a true California native, originally produced at Knott's Berry Farms when neighbor Rudolph Boysen showed them how to cross the blackberry, loganberry, and raspberry. The self-rising flour makes an especially light dumpling.

SERVES 6

1	lime
4	cups boysenberries
3	cups sliced peaches
½	cup plus 1 tablespoon sugar
½	teaspoon ground cinnamon
⅓	cup water
1	cup self-rising flour
3	tablespoons unsalted butter
2	large egg yolks
⅓	cup nonfat milk
	Whipped cream or vanilla ice cream

Grate the zest and juice the lime. Set the zest aside. Put the juice, berries, peaches, ½ cup of sugar, cinnamon, and water in a heavy 10- or 12-inch skillet. Cook over medium heat about 5 minutes or until the fruit is slightly soft and heated through.

Combine the flour, remaining sugar, and zest in a medium

bowl. Cut in the butter with a pastry blender or rub in with your fingers until the mixture resembles coarse crumbs. Beat the yolks and milk together in a measuring cup and stir into the flour just until blended. Do not overmix.

Bring the fruit mixture to a light boil over medium-high heat. Drop the batter by rounded tablespoons onto the boiling fruit, leaving a ½-inch border around the sides of the pan. Tightly cover the pan. Lower the heat to medium-low and simmer for 18 to 20 minutes. Do not uncover the pan while cooking.

Remove the pan from the heat. Remove the lid and cool the slump for 5 minutes. Spoon into dessert bowls and serve hot or warm with very lightly whipped cream or ice cream.

VARIATION

BLACKBERRY-APPLE SLUMP. Replace the lime with a lemon. Replace the boysenberries with blackberries and the peaches with Golden Delicious apples that have been peeled, cored, and sliced about ¼-inch thick. Increase the water to ½ cup or more if necessary. Proceed as above.

BLUEBERRY GRUNT

◆

B*lueberry grunt is a classic New England dessert, but any mixture of berries is equally delicious. The dumplings are a cross between a biscuit and a fluffy scone.*

SERVES 4

3 to 4	cups blueberries
½	cup plus 2 tablespoons sugar
I	cinnamon stick
I½	tablespoons orange zest
⅛ to ¼	teaspoon ground cloves or to taste
⅓ to ½	cup fresh orange juice
¼	cup water
½	cup all-purpose flour
I½	teaspoons baking powder
	Pinch of salt
I	large egg yolk
2 to 3	tablespoons buttermilk
	Heavy cream

Combine the blueberries, ½ cup of the sugar, cinnamon stick, zest, cloves, and juice in a heavy 2-quart saucepan over medium heat. (For a juicier slump add ¼ cup water to pan.) Simmer gently, about 5 minutes, until the berries are soft and juicy. Remove from the heat and discard the cinnamon.

Toss together the flour, baking powder, salt, and remaining sugar in a bowl. Lightly beat the yolk and buttermilk in a measuring cup with a fork. Stir into the flour and mix just until blended. Let batter sit a minute or two.

Drop the batter by half tablespoons on top of the berries, leaving about a ¼-inch border around the sides of the pan. Cover the pan tightly with the lid. Simmer over medium-low heat for 12 to 15 minutes, or until the dumplings are cooked through the center. Do not uncover the pan for 12 minutes. Remove from the heat. Serve hot or very warm with cream spooned on top.

VARIATION

MIXED BERRY SLUMP. Omit the cinnamon stick and ground cloves. Replace 1 cup of blueberries with 1 cup of blackberries and 1 cup of raspberries or use your favorite berry combination. Add 2 teaspoons finely chopped orange zest to the dumpling mixture. Proceed as above. You may need to add about ¼ cup water to the berries if there isn't enough juice.

NOTE: To double the dumplings use 3 tablespoons sugar, ⅛ teaspoon salt, 5 tablespoons of buttermilk, and double the remaining ingredients.

CRUMBLES, CRISPS,
AND BETTYS

◆

CHERRY-HAZELNUT OATMEAL CRUMBLE

◆

We prefer making this crumble with canned cherries
because of the amount of juice provided.

SERVES 6 TO 8

2	16-ounce cans pitted tart cherries
1 to 1½	cups granulated sugar
⅓	cup cornstarch
	Pinch of salt
¼	teaspoon almond extract
¾	cup all-purpose flour
¼	cup firmly packed light brown sugar
½	cup oatmeal
½	cup coarsely chopped hazelnuts or almonds
8	tablespoons (1 stick) unsalted butter, cut into pieces

Preheat the oven to 375° F.

Drain the cherries, reserving 1 cup of the juice. In a heavy
2-quart saucepan mix together ¾ cup of the sugar, the cornstarch, and salt. Slowly stir in the reserved juice. Cook over

medium-low heat, stirring constantly, until the mixture is thick and bubbly. Remove from the heat. Stir in the cherries, almond extract, and ¼ cup of granulated sugar or to taste. Spoon the mixture into a deep 1½-quart oval baking dish.

Toss together the flour, remaining sugars, oatmeal, and nuts in a bowl. Cut in the butter with a pastry blender or rub in with your fingers until the mixture resembles coarse crumbs. Sprinkle over the filling.

Bake 35 to 40 minutes, or until the crumble is bubbly at the edges and the topping is golden brown. Serve warm.

APPLE-CHEDDAR CRUMBLE

◆

There isn't a more perfect combination than apples and Cheddar—unless it's grapes and Brie. Use the best Cheddar available for the most buttery results. Packaged preshredded cheese will create a rubbery-textured topping.

SERVES 6

2   pounds tart green apples, peeled,
      cored, and sliced (5 to 5½ cups)
½   cup golden raisins
1   cup firmly packed light brown
      sugar
2   teaspoons ground cinnamon
1   teaspoon ground nutmeg
½   teaspoon ground cardamom
⅔   cup all-purpose flour
1¼ cups (5 ounces) finely shredded
      sharp Cheddar cheese, at room
      temperature
4   tablespoons (½ stick) cold unsalted
      butter, cut into 1-inch pieces
½   cup coarsely chopped pecans
      Crème Anglaise (page 117) or
      vanilla ice cream

Preheat the oven to 400° F.

Combine the apples, raisins, ⅔ cup of the brown sugar, and spices. Turn mixture into shallow 3-quart baking dish.

In a small bowl, combine the remaining sugar, the flour, and ¾ cup of the cheese. Cut in the butter with a pastry blender or rub in with your fingers until the mixture resembles coarse crumbs. Stir in the remaining cheese and pecans. Sprinkle over the apples.

Bake for 35 to 40 minutes, or until the apples are tender and juicy and the topping is golden. Let sit 5 minutes, then spoon into bowls and serve hot or warm with Crème Anglaise or ice cream.

AFTER-SCHOOL
DATE CRUMBLES

◆

These great after-school snacks were popular in the
1950s and 60s, when they were Mom's special treat. Try them with
a glass of passion fruit iced tea or cold milk.

MAKES 24 BARS

1½   cups pitted dates
1½   cups freshly squeezed orange juice
2½   cups all-purpose flour
1½   cups firmly packed light brown
     sugar
1½   cups (3 sticks) cold unsalted butter,
     cut into 1-inch pieces
1   cup sweetened flaked coconut
1   cup chopped walnuts
1½   cups rolled oats

Combine the dates and orange juice in a heavy saucepan over
low heat. Cook, stirring occasionally, until the mixture is
thickened, about 30 minutes.

Preheat the oven to 350° F.

Combine the flour and sugar in a medium bowl. Cut in
the butter with a pastry blender or rub in with your fingers

until the mixture resembles coarse crumbs. Stir in the remaining ingredients. Press half the dough into a 13 × 9 × 2-inch baking pan. Spread the date mixture over the dough to within ½ inch of the edges. Press the remaining dough over the date mixture.

Bake for 40 to 45 minutes, or until golden. Cool crumbles in the pan on a rack. Cut into bars. Serve warm or at room temperature.

VARIATION

◆

APPLE-CRANBERRY CRUMBLE SLICES. Omit dates and orange juice. Melt ½ cup of unsalted butter in a large skillet over medium heat. Add 10 cups peeled and sliced Golden Delicious apples (about 5) and 1 cup dried cranberries. Sprinkle with ¾ cup granulated sugar, 2 teaspoons ground cinnamon, 1 teaspoon ground nutmeg, ½ teaspoon ground cloves, and 2 teaspoons vanilla extract. Cook over medium heat, about 10 minutes, stirring occasionally until the apples are soft.

Make the dough as above, using ¾ cup of the sugar.

PEAR-CRANBERRY CRISP

◆

Start a new Thanksgiving or Christmas tradition by adding this light crisp to your holiday menu.

SERVES 6

2 **pounds Bosc or Anjou pears, peeled, cored, and sliced (about 5 cups)**
2 **cups fresh or frozen cranberries**
¼ **cup granulated sugar**
¾ **cup firmly packed light brown sugar**
¾ **cup all-purpose flour**
1 **teaspoon ground nutmeg**
8 **tablespoons (1 stick) cold unsalted butter, cut into 1-inch pieces**
1 **cup coarsely chopped hazelnuts (filberts)**
½ **cup quick-cooking oatmeal**
   Heavy cream or vanilla ice cream

Preheat the oven to 350° F.

Combine the pears and cranberries in a deep 1½- to 2-quart baking dish. Sprinkle the granulated sugar over the fruit and toss thoroughly.

Mix the brown sugar, flour, and nutmeg in a medium

38

bowl. Cut in the butter with a pastry blender or rub in with your fingers until the mixture resembles coarse crumbs. Mix in the nuts and oatmeal. Sprinkle evenly over the fruit.

Bake for 35 to 40 minutes, or until the fruit is bubbly and the top is golden brown. Spoon into bowls and serve hot or warm with heavy cream or ice cream.

APPLE, RHUBARB, AND FENNEL CRISP

◆

Fennel, *considered one of the nine sacred herbs by medieval Anglo-Saxon sages, is actually native to the Mediterranean and very popular in Italian and French cooking. The seeds impart a flavor similar to yet less powerful than anise.*

SERVES 6

8 tablespoons (I stick) plus 2 teaspoons cold unsalted butter, cut into pieces

2 pounds cooking apples, peeled and cut into ¼-inch slices (about 5½ cups)

I pound fresh rhubarb, washed, dried, and cut into I-inch slices (about 4 cups)

I tablespoon fresh lemon juice

½ cup granulated sugar, or to taste

2 tablespoons toasted fennel seeds, lightly crushed

I¼ cups all-purpose flour

I cup firmly packed light brown sugar

¾ teaspoon ground cinnamon
¼ teaspoon ground nutmeg
Sweetened whipped cream or
vanilla ice cream

Preheat the oven to 375° F. Butter an 8-inch square baking pan with 2 teaspoons of the butter.

Combine the apples, rhubarb, lemon juice, granulated sugar, fennel, and ¼ cup of the flour in a large bowl, then pour into the prepared pan.

Combine the remaining flour, the brown sugar, cinnamon, and nutmeg in a medium bowl. Cut in the remaining butter with a pastry blender or rub in with your fingers until the mixture forms coarse crumbs. Sprinkle over the fruit mixture.

Bake for 35 to 40 minutes or until the topping is deep golden brown and the filling bubbles. Serve warm with whipped cream or ice cream.

INDIVIDUAL HONEY
RHUBARB CRISPS

◆

Our friend George Morrone used to serve crisps similar to these when he was the chef at the Bel Air Hotel in California. The vanilla ice cream perfectly complements this not-so-sweet crisp.

SERVES 8

12 **tablespoons (1½ sticks) cold**
    unsalted butter
2½ **pounds rhubarb, washed, dried, and**
    cut into ½-inch slices (10 to 11
    cups)
1 **tablespoon grated lime zest**
⅓ **cup honey**
¾ **cup sugar**
¼ **cup firmly packed light brown**
    sugar
1 **cup bread flour or all-purpose flour**
    Vanilla ice cream

Preheat the oven to 375° F. Butter 8 earthenware ramekins with about 2 tablespoons of the butter.

Spoon the rhubarb into the ramekins, filling each about

two-thirds full. Combine the lime zest and honey in a measuring cup and drizzle about 2 teaspoons over each ramekin.

Combine the sugars and flour in a bowl. Cut in the remaining butter with a pastry blender or rub in with your fingers until the mixture resembles coarse crumbs. Fill the ramekins to the top with the mixture.

Bake 1 hour until the filling bubbles. Serve hot or warm with ice cream.

WHITE PEACH AND MANGO BETTY

◆

An elegant dessert for a special summer dinner.

SERVES 4 TO 6

4½	tablespoons unsalted butter, melted
2	pounds (6 medium) white peaches, peeled and sliced (4 to 5 cups)
2	large mangoes, peeled and cubed (about 2 cups)
2	tablespoons dark rum
2	tablespoons fresh lime juice
½ to ⅔	cup granulated sugar or to taste
2	cups coarsely ground zwieback (1 6-ounce box, 24 slices)
¼	cup firmly packed light brown sugar
1	teaspoon ground cinnamon
⅓	cup chopped pecans
	Vanilla or macadamia ice cream

Preheat the oven to 375° F. Lightly brush a 1-quart baking dish with 1 to 2 teaspoons of the melted butter.

In a large bowl, toss together the peaches, mangoes, rum, lime juice, and sugar to taste.

In a medium bowl, toss together the zwieback, brown sugar, and cinnamon. Stir in the remaining butter until the crumbs are lightly moistened.

Arrange half the fruit in the baking dish. Sprinkle half the crumbs over the fruit. Repeat the layers, ending with crumbs. Sprinkle with the pecans.

Bake for 40 to 45 minutes, or until the betty is bubbly at the edges. (Check after 25 minutes. If the crumbs are browning too quickly, lightly cover with aluminum foil.) Serve hot with ice cream.

VARIATION

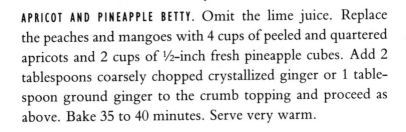

APRICOT AND PINEAPPLE BETTY. Omit the lime juice. Replace the peaches and mangoes with 4 cups of peeled and quartered apricots and 2 cups of ½-inch fresh pineapple cubes. Add 2 tablespoons coarsely chopped crystallized ginger or 1 tablespoon ground ginger to the crumb topping and proceed as above. Bake 35 to 40 minutes. Serve very warm.

AUTUMN HARVEST
BROWN BETTY

◆

A *little crunchier and more chewy than the usual betty, this dessert is similar to a crisp. Instead of the usual crumb topping, the crumbs and fruit are repeated in successive layers.*

SERVES 6

2 **cups Grape Nuts cereal**

½ **cup (1 stick) unsalted butter, melted**

2 **cups peeled and sliced tart apples**

2 **cups peeled and sliced pears (Anjou or Bosc)**

¾ **cup dried cranberries**

1 **tablespoon finely grated orange zest**

1 **teaspoon ground cinnamon**

½ **teaspoon ground nutmeg**

¼ **teaspoon ground allspice**

⅓ **cup freshly squeezed orange juice**

½ **cup firmly packed light brown sugar**

Heavy cream, vanilla ice cream, or Crème Anglaise (page 117)

Preheat the oven to 375° F.

In a medium bowl, combine the cereal with the butter and toss until well coated.

Put the apples, pears, and cranberries in another bowl. Sprinkle the zest and spices over the fruit, then add the orange juice and brown sugar. Lightly stir to coat the fruit.

Pat one-third of the cereal mixture on the bottom of a shallow 1½-quart baking dish. Layer half the fruit on top. Repeat the layering, finishing with the cereal. Cover with foil.

Bake for 40 minutes. Remove the foil, raise the heat to 400° F. and bake 12 to 15 minutes more. Cool for 5 to 10 minutes before serving with cream, ice cream, or Crème Anglaise.

VARIATION

◆

APPLE-RAISIN BREAD BETTY. Replace Grape Nuts cereal with 3 cups cinnamon-raisin bread cubes. Replace the orange juice with apple juice. Put half the fruit mixture on the bottom of the pan. Top with half the bread cubes. Repeat the layers. Bake and serve as above.

BOURBON PEAR BETTY

◆

A delicious quickly-put-together dessert that tastes even better the second day.

SERVES 8

2 cups dry white bread crumbs

½ cup butter, melted

12 medium Anjou or Bosc pears, peeled, cored, and sliced about ⅛-inch thick

2 tablespoons fresh lemon juice

½ cup granulated sugar

½ cup firmly packed light brown sugar

2 teaspoons ground cinnamon

½ teaspoon ground nutmeg

1 teaspoon finely grated lemon zest

½ cup bourbon

Preheat the oven to 375° F. Butter a deep 2-quart baking dish.

Toss the bread crumbs with the butter in a small bowl.

Place the pears in a large bowl and sprinkle with the lemon juice. Add the sugars, spices, and zest and toss well.

Sprinkle one-third of the crumbs over the bottom of the

baking dish. Spread half of the pear mixture on top. Repeat the layers, finishing with crumbs. Pour the bourbon over. Cover the dish with foil and make a few slits in the top.

Bake for 45 minutes. Uncover and bake for 15 minutes more or until the topping is golden brown. Serve warm or at room temperature.

DUMPLINGS, PIES,
AND TARTS

◆

SPICED APPLE DUMPLINGS WITH CHEDDAR PASTRY

◆

These dumplings can be prepared a day in advance and baked the next morning for a special breakfast treat.

SERVES 6

1	recipe Cheddar Pastry (page 114), unbaked
¼	cup raisins
¼	cup dark rum
⅓	cup firmly packed light brown sugar
¼	cup coarsely chopped almonds
1	teaspoon finely grated orange zest
3	teaspoons ground cinnamon
¼	teaspoon ground nutmeg
⅛	teaspoon ground cloves
6	medium-tart green apples (Pippins or Granny Smiths)
½	cup granulated sugar
3	tablespoons unsalted butter
1¼	cups Cinnamon Syrup (page 115)

Have 6 pastry squares ready in the refrigerator.

Combine the raisins and rum in a small bowl; let sit for at least 1 hour or overnight.

Preheat the oven to 425° F.

Drain the raisins and mix with the brown sugar, almonds, zest, 1 teaspoon of the cinnamon, and the nutmeg and cloves. Peel and core the apples. Mix the remaining cinnamon with the granulated sugar in a shallow bowl. Roll the apples in the cinnamon sugar until they are completely coated.

Place an apple in the center of each pastry square. Stuff each apple with 2 tablespoons of raisin filling and top with 1½ teaspoons butter. Lift the corners of pastry up to overlap the top of the apple and seal with moistened fingertips.

Place the dumplings in a large, shallow, oblong baking dish. Pour the syrup over the dumplings.

Bake for 45 to 50 minutes, or until golden brown and a metal skewer easily pierces the apples. (Check the dumplings periodically to make sure the syrup does not burn. If it becomes too dark, add some water to the pan.) Let the dumplings cool 15 to 20 minutes before serving. Spoon any remaining syrup over each and serve warm.

NECTARINE AND WILD
BLUEBERRY DUMPLINGS

◆

Frozen puff pastry makes these old-fashioned dumplings a light, more contemporary dessert, good for brunch.

SERVES 6 TO 8

2	sheets frozen puff pastry (17¼-ounce package), thawed
2	pounds ripe nectarines, diced and peeled (4 cups)
1	cup fresh or canned wild blueberries, drained
¾	cup dried wild blueberries
½	cup toasted chopped hazelnuts
⅓	cup firmly packed light brown sugar
1 to 1½	cups Cinnamon Syrup (page 115)
	Vanilla ice cream

Preheat the oven to 400° F. Lightly butter two 13 × 9 × 2-inch baking dishes.

On a lightly floured board, roll out the puff pastry to form two 12 × 14-inch rectangles.

Spread the pastry with half the nectarines, both kinds of

berries, and nuts. Sprinkle with 2½ tablespoons of the sugar. Starting on the longer side, roll the pastry up like a jelly roll and seal the edges with a little water. Cut into 2-inch slices. Repeat with the other pastry. Place the slices cut surface down in the baking dishes, being careful not to fit them in tightly. Pour about ½ to ¾ cup of the Cinnamon Syrup over the dumplings in each dish.

Bake for 40 to 45 minutes. Serve warm with ice cream and additional Cinnamon Syrup, if desired.

CONNIE BATES'S CHERRY PIE

◆

Our dear friend Connie Bates, who lives in the village of Waddington in Lancashire, England, serves this pie with lots of thick double cream.

SERVES 4 to 6

1	recipe Connie's Pie Crust (page 112), unbaked
4 to 5	cups pitted fresh tart cherries, or 4 cups canned Morello cherries, drained
1	small cooking apple, peeled, cored, and coarsely chopped
2 to 4	tablespoons water or cherry juice
½ to ¾	cup sugar or honey, to taste
	Cold Crème Anglaise (page 117) or heavy cream

Prepare the crust and lattice strips; refrigerate until ready to use.

Preheat the oven to 375° F.

Over medium heat in a medium saucepan, combine the cherries, apples, and water or cherry juice. Cook until the fruit is soft, about 10 minutes. Add the sugar or honey to taste depending on the tartness of the cherries and cook a few more minutes until the juices have thickened. Cool a few minutes, then pour into the pie shell. Moisten the rim of the pastry around the edges.

Weave the pastry strips into a lattice over the pie and seal by pinching the ends to the bottom crust. Bake for 25 to 30 minutes until the top crust is golden brown.

Serve hot or warm with cold Crème Anglaise or heavy cream poured on top of individual servings.

DEEP-DISH CINNAMON APPLE PIE

◆

The best apple pie ever.

SERVES 8

1	recipe All-Purpose Fruit Pie Crust (page 110), unbaked
3½	pounds tart green apples, peeled, cored, and sliced about ¼-inch thick (9 cups)
1½	cups golden raisins
1	cup sugar
1	tablespoon fresh lemon juice
4	teaspoons ground cinnamon
1½	teaspoons ground nutmeg
¾	teaspoon ground mace
½	teaspoon ground allspice
3	tablespoons unsalted butter, cut into pieces
½	teaspoon ground cinnamon mixed with 2 tablespoons sugar
	Sharp Cheddar cheese or vanilla ice cream

Chill the 10-inch prepared shell and top crust for 10 minutes. Preheat the oven to 425° F.

In a large bowl, combine the apples, raisins, sugar, lemon juice, and spices. Pile into the chilled shell. Dot with the butter. Moisten the edge of the bottom pastry with cold water. Cover with the top crust. Trim to a ½-inch overhang. Fold the edge over the bottom crust overhang, then press the dough together making a raised ridge around the rim. Flute with your fingers or seal with the tines of a fork.

Cut 3 or 4 vents in the center of the pie. Sprinkle the top with the cinnamon sugar.

Bake on a cookie sheet in the lower third of the oven for 55 to 60 minutes. Check halfway through to make sure the crust is not browning too quickly. If it is, cover with a strip of aluminum foil around the edges.

Remove to a wire rack. Serve hot, warm, or at room temperature with slices of Cheddar or with ice cream.

FLOATING LEMON
SPONGE PIE

◆

This sturdy heirloom dessert can be baked in a pie shell as it's done in the South, or in a buttered 1½-quart baking dish as they do up North. Vary the flavor by substituting limes or oranges, or by combining any of your favorite citrus fruits. For beautiful color, try combining blood orange and lemon juice.

SERVES 6

½	recipe All-Purpose Fruit Pie Crust (page 110), unbaked
2	tablespoons unsalted butter, softened
⅔ to 1	cup sugar
2	large eggs, separated
¼	cup fresh lemon juice
2	teaspoons grated lemon zest
3	tablespoons all-purpose flour
1	cup cold milk
	Confectioners' sugar
	Mint sprigs or candied violets

Preheat the oven to 425° F.

Line a 9-inch pie pan with the crust and lightly prick the bottom all over with a fork. Bake for 10 minutes. Set aside until ready to use. Lower the heat to 350° F.

Cream the butter with ⅔ to 1 cup of sugar, depending on your taste, and egg yolks in a medium bowl. Beat in the juice, zest, and flour. Stir in the milk. In another bowl, beat the egg whites until stiff. Gently fold into the lemon mixture. Pour into the pie shell.

Bake 35 to 45 minutes, or until the filling is set and golden brown. Before serving, sprinkle each slice with a little confectioners' sugar and decorate with mint sprigs or candied violets. Serve warm, at room temperature, or cold.

NORTHWEST
BLACKBERRY-LIME PIE

◆

This pie is especially delicious when made with wild
Northwestern blackberries.

SERVES 6

| 1 | recipe All-Purpose Fruit Pie Crust
  (page 110), unbaked |
| 1 | large or extra-large egg yolk |
| ½ | tablespoon water |
| 6 | cups washed and drained
  blackberries |
2	tablespoons fresh lime juice
1	teaspoon lime zest
1 to 2	tablespoons sugar, to taste
½	cup all-purpose flour
	Sweetened whipped cream flavored
with 2 tablespoons vanilla extract,
or vanilla ice cream

Prepare the double crust for a 9- to 10-inch pie pan. Set the
top crust aside. Line the bottom of the pan with the other
crust. Beat together the yolk and water. Brush on the bottom crust. Set aside.

Preheat the oven to 400° F. Combine the blackberries, juice, zest, sugar to taste, and flour. Pour into the pie shell.

Moisten the edge of the shell with cold water. Cover with the top crust. Trim to a ½-inch overhang. Fold the edge over the bottom crust overhang, then press the dough together making a raised ridge around the rim. Flute with your fingers or seal with the tines of a fork.

Brush the top crust with the remaining egg wash. Cut 3 to 4 vents in the center of the pie.

Bake on a cookie sheet in the lower third of the oven for 40 minutes. Check halfway through to make sure the crust is not browning too quickly. If it is, cover the crust with aluminum foil.

Cool on a wire rack. Serve warm with sweetened whipped cream or ice cream.

STRAWBERRY GLACÉ TART

◆

Strawberries are usually used in this classic summer
dessert, but any berries in season will be just as irresistible.

SERVES 6

½ recipe for Easy Cream Cheese
   Pastry (page 108), unbaked
6 cups whole medium strawberries,
   cleaned and hulled
¾ cup sugar or to taste
3 tablespoons cornstarch
½ cup water
1 3-ounce package of cream cheese,
   at room temperature
1 to 2 tablespoons milk
   Sweetened whipped cream

Preheat the oven to 425° F.

Line a 9-inch tart or pie pan with the crust and prick the
bottom all over with a fork. Bake for 15 to 20 minutes, until
just pale golden. Set aside until ready to use.

Mash enough strawberries to make 1 cup of puree. Mix
the sugar with the cornstarch in a 2-quart saucepan. Stir in
the water and strawberries. Cook over medium heat, stirring
occasionally, until the mixture boils and thickens. Stirring

constantly, boil 1 minute more. Immediately remove from the heat.

Beat the cream cheese with enough milk for a smooth, creamy consistency. Spread on the bottom of the tart shell. Fill the shell with the remaining whole strawberries, placing them hulled side down. Pour the berry mixture on top. Chill at least 3 hours or until set. Serve cold with whipped cream.

ALL-AMERICAN
RASPBERRY-BLUEBERRY
CHEESECAKE TART

◆

This dish requires less work than it seems. The pre-baked shell, or the whole pie, can be baked in advance and frozen. Decorate the frozen tart with the fresh fruit several hours before serving. Any fresh fruit is delicious with the filling.

SERVES 8

1 **recipe for Sweet Pastry (page 107)**
⅔ **cup currant jelly, melted**
1 **8-ounce package cream cheese, at
  room temperature**
⅓ **cup sugar**
6 **tablespoons (¾ stick) unsalted
  butter, at room temperature**
2 **large eggs, at room temperature**
¼ **cup fresh lemon juice**
3 **tablespoons grated lemon peel**
⅛ **teaspoon freshly grated nutmeg**
1 **cup raspberries**
2 **cups blueberries**
  Sweetened whipped cream

Have the baked tart shell ready.

Preheat the oven to 350° F. With a pastry brush, evenly coat the bottom of the tart shell with ⅓ cup of the jelly.

In a large mixing bowl, beat the cream cheese, sugar, and butter until very smooth. Add the eggs, one at a time, blending well after each addition. Stir in lemon juice, grated zest, and nutmeg. Pour into the tart shell. Bake for 25 minutes or until set. Cool completely on a wire rack. Remove tart pan ring.

Arrange a border of raspberries around the tart. Fill the center with the blueberries. Bring the remaining jelly to a boil over medium heat. Brush the fruit lightly with the jelly.

Chill the tart until ready to serve. Serve with dollops of whipped cream.

BANBERRY TARTS

◆

We know the town of Banbury, England, would definitely approve of the liberties we've taken with their famous turnovers.

ABOUT 12 TO 15 TARTS

1   recipe for Easy Cream Cheese
    Pastry (page 108), unbaked
1   cup dried cranberries or dried tart
    cherries
¼   cup golden raisins
¾   cup sugar
½   teaspoon ground nutmeg
½   cup water
⅓   cup freshly squeezed orange juice
2   tablespoons fresh lemon juice
1½ tablespoons unsalted butter
1½ tablespoons fine cracker crumbs or
    matzo meal
1   tablespoon grated orange zest
1   large egg, lightly beaten
    Confectioners' sugar
    Mild English Cheddar or Cheshire
    cheese

Preheat the oven to 425° F.

Roll out the pastry to ⅛-inch thick. Cut into 4-inch squares or circles. Refrigerate until ready to use.

Combine the cranberries or cherries, raisins, sugar, nutmeg, water, and juices in a medium saucepan. Cover and simmer over medium heat for 10 minutes or until the fruit is soft. Remove from the heat and stir in the butter, crumbs or meal, and orange zest. Let cool.

Stir the egg into the fruit. Place about 1 tablespoon of filling on each piece of pastry. Fold the pastry over the filling to form a triangle or half-circle. Moisten the edges of the pastry with a little water, then seal tightly by pressing the edges together with a fork dipped in flour. Prick the top of the pastry a few times with the fork. Lift the tarts off the working surface with a spatula and transfer to an ungreased cookie sheet.

Bake until lightly browned, about 15 to 20 minutes. Serve warm with a dusting of confectioners' sugar and Cheddar or Cheshire cheese.

PEAR TURNOVERS

◆

Turnovers are nothing more than little "handpies" that are great travelers. Keep a batch frozen for your next picnic or potluck.

SERVES 6

1	recipe for Easy Cream Cheese Pastry (page 108)
4	cups (about 2 pounds) ripe pears, peeled, cored, and cut into ¼-inch slices
⅓	cup dried currants
¾	cup firmly packed light brown sugar
3	tablespoons cornstarch
2	tablespoons Amaretto
1⅛	teaspoons cinnamon
2	tablespoons granulated sugar

Preheat the oven to 400° F.

Divide the pastry dough into 6 equal pieces. With a lightly floured rolling pin, roll each piece of dough on a lightly floured surface to form an 8-inch square. Set aside.

Combine the pears, currants, brown sugar, cornstarch, Amaretto, and 1 teaspoon of the cinnamon in a bowl. Spread

½ cup of filling on each square, leaving a ¾-inch border. Fold the pastry over the filling to form a triangle. Moisten the edges of the pastry with a little water, then press the edges together with a fork to seal tightly. Make three slits in the top of each turnover. Sprinkle with remaining cinnamon mixed with the granulated sugar. Place the turnovers on an ungreased cookie sheet.

Bake for 20 to 25 minutes, or until golden brown. Remove from the pan and cool on wire racks. Serve warm or at room temperature.

NOTE: To bake frozen, place turnovers on an ungreased cookie sheet and bake in a preheated 425° F. oven until golden brown, about 20 to 25 minutes.

SHORTCAKES,
BATTER CAKES,
AND BUCKLES

◆

WARM RHUBARB
SHORTCAKES

◆

These shortcake biscuits freeze very well. The dough, similar to that for scones, should be handled as little as possible to ensure a light and delicate cake.

6 TO 8 SHORTCAKES

2	pounds fresh rhubarb, cut into 1-inch pieces (8 cups)
1½ to 2⅓	cups granulated sugar
1	cup fresh orange juice
2	cups all-purpose flour
2½	teaspoons baking powder
½	teaspoon baking soda
½	teaspoon salt
1	tablespoon finely grated orange zest
6	tablespoons cold unsalted butter, cut into pieces
1	large egg
2½	cups heavy cream
1	cup Hot Butterscotch Sauce (page 118)

Preheat the oven to 350° F.

Combine the rhubarb, 1½ to 2 cups of the sugar or to taste, and orange juice in a 3-quart baking dish. Cover and bake for 20 to 30 minutes or until the rhubarb is tender. Do not stir; the fruit should retain its shape. Set aside and keep warm.

Raise the oven heat to 400° F. Combine the flour, ⅓ cup of the sugar, baking powder, soda, salt, and zest in a large bowl. Cut in the butter with a pastry blender or rub in with your fingers until the mixture resembles coarse crumbs. Lightly beat the egg with ⅓ cup of the cream in a small bowl. Stir into the flour mixture with a fork. Add 1 to 2 tablespoons of additional cream to work into a moist dough.

Turn the dough onto a lightly floured board. Gently knead 8 to 10 strokes. Sprinkle with a little flour and with floured fingertips pat the dough into a round about ¾-inch thick. Cut with a round 2½-inch floured cookie cutter. Combine the scraps and repeat. Place the shortcakes on a lightly greased cookie sheet. Brush the tops with a little cream.

Bake for 10 to 12 minutes or until light golden brown and firm. Cover to keep warm.

To serve, whip the remaining cream just until very soft peaks form. Split the warm shortcakes in half. Place the bottom halves on individual plates. Spoon some warm rhubarb over. Top with a dollop of whipped cream and cover with other half of the cake. Top with more rhubarb and another dollop of cream. Spoon 1½ to 2 tablespoons Hot Butterscotch Sauce over. Serve immediately.

BETTER-THAN-BEST OLD-FASHIONED STRAWBERRY SHORTCAKE

◆

This shortcake dough can be made ahead, wrapped in plastic wrap, and stored in the refrigerator for up to two days, or frozen for one month.

SERVES 6 TO 8

9	tablespoons cold unsalted butter, cut into pieces
2½	cups all-purpose flour, sifted
½	cup superfine sugar
4	teaspoons baking powder
½	teaspoon cream of tartar
¼	teaspoon ground nutmeg
	Pinch of salt
2	large egg yolks, lightly beaten
⅓	cup milk or half-and-half
2	pints (about 1½ pounds) fresh strawberries, sliced
2	cups sweetened whipped cream

Preheat the oven to 450° F. Grease two 8-inch cake pans with 1 tablespoon of the butter.

Combine the flour with ¼ cup of the sugar, and the baking powder, cream of tartar, nutmeg, and salt in a medium bowl. Cut in the remaining butter with a pastry blender or rub in with your fingers until the mixture resembles coarse crumbs. Add the egg yolks and milk and stir until a soft dough forms. Divide the dough in half, and with floured fingertips pat into the cake pans. Sprinkle 1 tablespoon of the sugar over each shortcake.

Bake for 10 to 12 minutes until light golden. Cool in the pans on a wire rack for 10 minutes, then invert onto the rack.

Meanwhile, put the berries in a bowl and sprinkle with the remaining 2 tablespoons of sugar or to taste. Lightly mix with a fork, crushing some of the berries to release the juice as you mix. Taste and adjust the sugar if necessary.

Immediately before serving, spread half the whipped cream over the top of one cake. Arrange half the berries over the cream. Top with the second shortcake and repeat the layers. Cut into wedges and serve.

VARIATION

CHOCOLATE STRAWBERRY SHORTCAKES. Add ¼ to ⅓ cup grated bittersweet chocolate to the dry ingredients and proceed as above.

PINEAPPLE–MACADAMIA NUT UPSIDE-DOWN CAKE

◆

The pineapple was offered by the West Indians as a sign of hospitality when the first Spanish explorers came to the Americas. Serve this version of an old favorite and you're sure to prove the natives knew what they were talking about . . . pineapplewise, that is.

SERVES 6

4	tablespoons plus ⅓ cup unsalted butter, at room temperature
2 to 2½	cups fresh pineapple chunks (about half of 1 medium pineapple)
½	cup firmly packed dark brown sugar
1½	tablespoons coarsely chopped crystallized ginger
¾	cup granulated sugar
1	large egg, at room temperature
1	teaspoon vanilla extract
1½	cups cake flour
1½	teaspoons baking powder
½	teaspoon salt
½	cup plus 2 tablespoons milk
½	cup finely chopped macadamia nuts

Preheat the oven to 350° F.

Melt 4 tablespoons of the butter in an 8- or 9-inch square baking pan or a cast-iron skillet. Add the pineapple and sauté about 5 minutes or until tender. Sprinkle the brown sugar over the pineapple. Stir to melt some of the sugar. Neatly arrange the pineapple on the bottom of the pan. Sprinkle the ginger around the pineapple chunks.

Cream the granulated sugar and remaining ⅓ cup butter in a mixing bowl until light and fluffy. Beat in the egg. Stir in the vanilla. In another bowl, combine the flour, baking powder, and salt. Alternately add the dry ingredients and the milk to the egg mixture, mixing well after each addition. Fold in the nuts. Pour batter over the pineapple chunks and spread evenly with the back of a wooden spoon or spatula.

Bake for 35 minutes, or until the cake springs back when lightly touched and a cake tester inserted in center comes out clean. Loosen the cake around the edges with a knife and immediately invert onto a serving platter. Serve warm or at room temperature.

OKTOBERFEST APPLE HARVEST CAKE

◆

More *fruit than batter, this very moist snack cake travels well. It's the perfect dessert to pack in the lunch box or take to an autumn picnic or potluck dinner. Make it a day or two in advance so the flavors can mellow.*

SERVES 12

2	teaspoons unsalted butter or vegetable shortening
1⅓	pounds tart apples, cored, peeled, and sliced about ¼-inch thick (about 4 cups)
1	cup coarsely chopped walnuts
1½	cups sugar
2	cups all-purpose flour
2	teaspoons ground cinnamon
1½	teaspoons baking soda
½	teaspoon salt
2	large eggs, well beaten
¾	cup vegetable oil
2	teaspoons vanilla extract
	Confectioners' sugar

Preheat the oven to 350° F. Lightly grease the bottom and sides of a 13 × 9 × 2-inch cake pan with the butter or shortening. Line the bottom of the pan with baker's parchment or brown wrapping paper.

Toss the apples and nuts with the sugar in a large bowl. In another bowl, combine the flour, cinnamon, soda, and salt. Beat in the eggs, oil, and vanilla until the batter is thoroughly moistened. Pour the batter over the apples. Stir with a wooden spoon to evenly distribute the fruit (do not overmix) and pour into the pan.

Bake for 45 to 50 minutes or until a cake tester inserted in the center comes out clean. Cool in the pan for 15 minutes. Just before serving, sprinkle with confectioners' sugar and cut into 12 squares. Serve warm or at room temperature.

BLUEBERRY
GINGERBREAD BUCKLE

◆

A layer of caramelized blueberries tops this buckle, which is laden with whole blueberries and has a hint of crystallized ginger.

SERVES 8

¾ cup (1½ sticks) unsalted butter

1 cup firmly packed brown sugar

3 cups fresh blueberries

1 large egg

½ cup cold strong freshly brewed coffee

½ cup dark molasses

1¼ cups plus 2 tablespoons cake flour

1 teaspoon baking soda

¼ teaspoon salt

1 teaspoon ground ginger

½ teaspoon ground cinnamon

¼ teaspoon ground allspice

1 tablespoon finely grated lemon zest

2 tablespoons finely chopped
crystallized ginger
Lime Crème Fraîche (page 116) or
vanilla ice cream

Preheat the oven to 350° F.

Melt ¼ cup of the butter and pour into an 8-inch square baking pan. Add ½ cup of the brown sugar, stirring until smooth. Spread the mixture evenly over the bottom of the pan. Arrange 2 cups of the blueberries over the sugar. Set aside while you make the batter.

Cream the remaining butter and sugar in a large bowl until light and fluffy. Beat in the egg, then the coffee and molasses. In a separate bowl, combine 1¼ cups of the cake flour, soda, salt, spices, and zest. Stir into the molasses mixture. Toss the remaining 1 cup of blueberries and the ginger with the remaining flour in a small bowl. Gently fold into the batter. Spread the batter evenly over the blueberries in the pan.

Bake for 35 to 45 minutes, or until the cake springs back when lightly touched. Loosen the cake around the edges with a knife and immediately invert it onto a serving platter. Serve warm topped with Lime Crème Fraîche or ice cream.

CHERRY-ALMOND BUCKLE

◆

*A*ny *tart berries, such as cranberries, can be used instead of cherries.*

SERVES 6

6 tablespoons unsalted butter

1½ cups plus 2 tablespoons all-purpose flour

1 cup sugar

1 tablespoon cornstarch

1 16-ounce can (2 cups) Morello or sour red pie cherries, drained and juice reserved (about ¾ cup)

½ teaspoon almond extract

1 large egg, lightly beaten

2½ teaspoons baking powder
Pinch of salt

1 cup milk

½ cup sliced blanched almonds
Sweetened whipped cream or Crème Anglaise (page 117)

Preheat the oven to 350° F. Grease an 8- or 9-inch square baking pan with 2 teaspoons of the butter, then dust with 2 tablespoons of the flour, shaking off any excess. Set aside.

Mix ½ cup of the sugar with the cornstarch in a medium saucepan. Slowly stir in the reserved cherry juice to dissolve the cornstarch. Cook over medium heat, stirring constantly, until the mixture begins to boil and thicken slightly. Remove from the heat. Stir in 1 tablespoon of the butter and the almond extract. Stir in the cherries.

Beat the remaining sugar and butter in a large bowl until very light and fluffy. Beat in the egg. Sift together the remaining flour, baking powder, and salt. Alternately add the flour and milk, a third at a time, to the butter mixture, stirring after each addition, until completely blended. Pour into the prepared pan. Scatter the cherry mixture over the batter and sprinkle with the almonds.

Bake for 30 to 35 minutes or until a cake tester inserted into the center comes out clean. Serve warm with sweetened whipped cream or Crème Anglaise.

RED AND GREEN
GRAPE BUCKLE

◆

An icy glass of any sweet dessert wine is a perfect accompaniment to this very grapey and delicious buckle.

SERVES 6

10	tablespoons unsalted butter
3	cups red and green seedless grapes, washed and stemmed
¾	cup firmly packed light brown sugar
½	cup white grape juice
½	cup granulated sugar
3	large eggs, lightly beaten
1½	cups all-purpose flour
1	tablespoon baking powder
⅓	cup fresh lemon juice
	Sweetened whipped cream or Crème Fraîche, (page 116)

Preheat the oven to 350° F. Grease an 8-inch square baking pan with 1 tablespoon butter.

In a heavy 2-quart saucepan, combine the grapes, brown sugar, grape juice, and 3 tablespoons of the butter. Cook until the sugar has dissolved and the butter is melted. Set aside while you make the batter.

Melt the remaining butter. Mix with the granulated sugar. Beat in the eggs. Combine the flour and baking powder. Alternately add with the lemon juice to the butter mixture, stirring after each addition until well blended. Pour into the baking pan. Pour the grape mixture on top of the batter evenly.

Bake for 30 minutes or until a cake tester inserted in the center comes out clean. Serve hot or very warm with whipped cream or Crème Fraîche.

FRITTERS, FOOLS, AND OTHER FRUIT FAVORITES

◆

PAPAYA FRITTERS

◆

This is a variation of a dessert we had at the elegant
Bel Air Hotel in Bel Air, California. The batter, like a sweet
tempura, is delicious with any soft fruit, such as mangoes, peaches,
or nectarines.

SERVES 6

2	medium lemons
1	medium lime
1	medium orange
¾	cup milk
3	tablespoons unsalted butter, melted
1	teaspoon vanilla extract
1	large egg yolk
2	large egg whites
1	cup cake flour
2	tablespoons sugar
1	teaspoon ground nutmeg
¼	teaspoon salt
3	medium papayas, peeled, halved, and seeded
	Vegetable oil for frying
½ to ⅔	cup Lime Crème Fraîche (page 116)

Slice off the ends of one lemon, the lime, and the orange. With a potato peeler, carefully remove the peel from each in as long a strip as possible, making sure no white pith is included. Reserve fruit for another use. Cut peel into very thin julienne strips. Place in a bowl of cold water to cover and reserve. Grate the other lemon for 2 teaspoons of zest.

Combine the milk with the butter, vanilla, and lemon zest. Beat in the egg yolk. Sift the flour, sugar, nutmeg, and salt together and stir into the milk mixture. Beat the egg whites until stiff peaks form and gently fold into the batter. Do not overmix.

Fill a 10- or 12-inch heavy skillet with about 1 inch of oil. Heat to 375° F. Cut the papayas lengthwise into ¼-inch thick strips and dip into the batter, lightly coating them. Fry in batches until golden brown (about 3 minutes), turning them once. Carefully remove with a slotted spoon and drain on paper towels. Drain the julienne strips and blot dry with paper towels.

Arrange 6 or 7 fritters in a concentric circle on each serving plate. Place a dollop of Lime Crème Fraîche in the center of the circle. Sprinkle with a little of the julienne.

GOOSEBERRY FOOL

◆

Gooseberries were the Victorians' favorite fruit,
which they flavored with elderflowers to give a slight taste of muscat
grapes.

SERVES 4

2	cups green gooseberries, topped and tailed
½ to 1	cup sugar
¼	cup water
2	tablespoons Cassis
1	cup Crème Fraîche (page 116) or heavy cream

Combine the gooseberries, ¼ cup of the sugar, water, and
Cassis in a heavy nonreactive saucepan over medium heat.
Bring to a boil. Reduce the heat and simmer for 5 to 8 min-
utes until the fruit is soft and pulpy.

Puree the mixture in a blender or food processor, then pass
through a food mill. Return to the saucepan and cook 1 to 2
minutes until thick. Remove from the heat and cool completely. Taste for sweetness, adding sugar if necessary.

Beat the Crème Fraîche or cream with remaining sugar in
a chilled bowl with chilled beaters until soft peaks form.

Swirl in the fruit puree. Cover the bowl and allow to chill for at least 2 hours.

When ready to serve, pile the fool into custard cups or wineglasses. Accompany with shortbread or butter cookies.

VARIATION
◆

FRESH BERRY FOOL. Omit the water and Cassis. Replace the gooseberries with 1½ to 2 cups of mixed fresh berries—blackberries, raspberries, strawberries, blueberries, black currants, or even cranberries—and puree. Adjust the sugar as needed. Beat the Crème Fraîche as above and swirl in the uncooked puree. Chill and garnish with whole berries.

FROSTY MANGO FOOL

◆

When preparing this recipe in advance, remove the fools from the freezer 15 minutes before serving.

SERVES 4 TO 6

1   **extra-large egg white, at room temperature**
¼   **cup sugar or to taste**
1   **cup Crème Fraîche (page 116) or heavy cream**
1   **tablespoon fresh lime juice**
2   **cups fresh mango puree**

Beat the egg white with 1 teaspoon of the sugar until stiff in a small bowl. Beat the Crème Fraîche or cream in a chilled bowl with chilled beaters, gradually adding the remaining sugar, until soft peaks form. Stir the lime juice into the mango puree, then swirl into the whipped Crème Fraîche or cream. Fold in the egg white.

Spoon into custard cups. Freeze for about 1 hour or until thoroughly chilled but not frozen solid.

PINEAPPLE–BLOOD ORANGE AMBROSIA

◆

This is one of our favorite variations of ambrosia, a classic Victorian dessert.

SERVES 6

- 2 cups ½-inch fresh pineapple chunks
- 2 large blood oranges, peeled, segmented, and cut into ½-inch chunks
- 1 large Valencia orange, peeled, segmented, and cut into ½-inch chunks
- ½ cup grated fresh coconut, or unsweetened packaged
- ¼ cup sifted confectioners' sugar
- ¼ cup fresh lime juice
- 2 to 3 tablespoons Curaçao, to taste
- 18 large black cherries, pitted
  Pineapple sherbet or sorbet

Mix the pineapple, oranges, and coconut in a serving bowl. Sprinkle with the confectioners' sugar, lime juice, and Curaçao and toss gently. Chill 3 to 4 hours or overnight. Serve in goblets garnished with black cherries and pineapple sherbet or sorbet.

SPICED PEAR PUFF

◆

When *clafoutis, a classic French country dessert, incorporates Asian spices, it offers a completely new taste. Five-spice powder is available at most markets and in specialty stores.*

SERVES 6 TO 8

1¾	teaspoons five-spice powder
¾	cup sugar
4	tablespoons unsalted butter
2	cups peeled, cored, and thinly sliced ripe Bosc or Anjou pears
⅓	cup coarsely chopped crystallized ginger
3	large eggs
1¼	cups milk
1½	teaspoons vanilla
⅔	cup all-purpose flour

Preheat the oven to 375° F.

Combine the spice powder with ¼ cup of the sugar in a measuring cup. Melt 2 tablespoons of the butter in a skillet. Add the pears, half of the spice-sugar mixture, and the ginger. Toss well to coat the pears. Sauté just until the pears are tender, about 2 minutes.

Place the remaining butter in a 10- to 12-inch deep-dish

pie pan and melt in the oven. Whisk together the eggs, milk, and vanilla in a mixing bowl. Whisk in the remaining sugar. Whisk in half the flour, blending until smooth. Repeat with the remaining flour. Remove the pan from the oven. Carefully pour in the batter, then evenly distribute the pear mixture on top. Sprinkle with the remaining spice-sugar.

Bake for 45 minutes or until golden brown and puffy. Serve hot or warm.

BAKED APPLES WITH
DATE-NUT FILLING

◆

Rome Beauties (Red Rome) are the best apples for baking because they hold their shape when cooked, but Golden Delicious, Granny Smith, and Pippin varieties are also good baked.

SERVES 6

1 to 2	cups apple juice
½	cup sugar
6	large red apples
¼	cup gingersnap crumbs
¼	cup chopped walnuts
¼	cup chopped dates
2	tablespoons unsalted butter
1	cup heavy cream

Preheat the oven to 375° F.

Combine 1 cup of the apple juice and the sugar in a small saucepan. Cook over medium-high heat about 5 minutes, stirring until the sugar dissolves. Set aside.

Pare the apples about 1½ inches from the stem end. Carefully core to within ½ inch of the other end.

Combine the crumbs, nuts, and dates in a small bowl.

Stuff each apple with an equal quantity of the mixture and top with 1 teaspoon of butter.

Arrange the apples in a 9 × 13 × 2-inch baking dish. Pour the reserved syrup over and around the apples.

Bake for about 45 minutes to 1 hour, or until the apples are soft and sticky, basting frequently with the remaining apple juice. Transfer the apples to individual serving bowls.

Strain the baking juices into a saucepan. Place over low heat and reduce to about ½ cup. Do not boil or let the juices caramelize. Cool slightly, then whisk into the cream.

Serve immediately with some sauce spooned over each apple, or pass the sauce separately.

PEPPERED PEARS
IN RED WINE

◆

Deep ruby-colored poached pears scented with a peppery mixture of spices are elegant and impressive and, best of all, almost effortless to prepare. In the summer, replace the pears with firm peaches.

SERVES 2 TO 4

2 to 4	Bosc pears (not too ripe), peeled, with stems left on
1	bottle good-quality Pinot Noir or Beaujolais
½	cup port
½	cup sugar
4	whole cloves
3	whole star anise
1	tablespoon black peppercorns
1	cinnamon stick
1	vanilla bean, split
2 to 4	ounces Camembert or Gorgonzola cheese

Cut a thin slice from the bottom of each pear so it will sit straight on a plate.

Combine all the remaining ingredients, except the cheese, in a pot that is large enough to hold the pears but will allow them to be completely covered with liquid. Add the pears, cover, and bring to a simmer over medium heat. Cook 30 to 45 minutes, or until cooked through but still firm. Using a slotted spoon, remove the pears to a large shallow bowl. Cool to room temperature.

Over medium-high heat, reduce the cooking liquid to about ¾ to ½ cup syrup. Strain it over the pears. Refrigerate the pears in the liquid overnight.

Serve cold with Camembert or Gorgonzola that has been brought to room temperature.

NOTE: If the pears are prepared several days in advance (the flavor continues to improve), occasionally turn them in the syrup.

"HOT" BANANA SPLIT À LA YANKS

◆

One night, after dinner at Yanks in Beverly Hills, we were talked into ordering a banana split. What came to the table was an enormous surprise that easily could have fed six. But the two of us had no problem polishing it off. Our recipe approximates the dish. Use a store-bought "gourmet" brand of fudge sauce or your favorite recipe.

SERVES 2

- 2 large ripe bananas, unpeeled
- 1 scoop each vanilla, espresso, and double-fudge high-quality ice cream
- ¼ cup hot fudge sauce
- ¼ cup Hot Butterscotch Sauce (page 118)
- ½ cup whipped cream
- ¼ cup blueberries
- ¼ cup raspberries
- ¼ cup strawberries, hulled and halved
- 2 tablespoons chopped pecans
  Mint sprig for garnish

Preheat the oven to 325° F.

Roast the bananas in their skins for about 10 minutes. Cool slightly, peel, and slice lengthwise.

Place 1 large scoop of each ice cream in a soup bowl. Surround the ice cream with the banana slices. Heat the hot fudge sauce according to the directions on the label or pour into a double boiler and slowly heat until desired temperature. Do the same with the butterscotch sauce. Drizzle each over the ice cream. Top with the whipped cream. Strew the fresh berries over, then sprinkle on the pecans. Garnish with mint sprig.

GINGERED RHUBARB AND STRAWBERRY COMPOTE

◆

The perfect ending to a summer lunch.

SERVES 6

½ **cup water**

I **cup sugar**

I **2-inch piece fresh ginger, peeled and quartered**

I **pound fresh rhubarb, peeled and cut**
   into I ½-inch pieces (about 4 cups)

I **tablespoon orange zest**

I **pint medium strawberries, hulled and halved**

I **tablespoon kirsch (optional)**
   Heavy cream

Bring the water, sugar, and ginger to a boil in a heavy sauce-pan over medium heat. Add the rhubarb, bring back to boil-ing, then lower the heat. Partially cover and simmer for 3 to 4 minutes or until the fruit is soft but retains its shape. Re-move from the heat. Gently stir in the orange zest. Cool the mixture to room temperature and stir in the strawberries and kirsch. Chill.

Remove the ginger before serving in goblets topped with heavy cream.

BLUEBERRY FLUMMERY

◆

Flummeries are highly favored in New England. Traditional recipes call for cornstarch, but we prefer using farina, which produces a more substantial texture.

SERVES 4

3	cups blueberries
⅓	cup sugar
1	cup white or purple grape juice
½	teaspoon grated orange zest
4	tablespoons instant farina, such as Cream of Wheat
1 to 1½	cups heavy cream

Combine blueberries, sugar, and grape juice in a medium nonreactive saucepan. Cook over medium heat until the berries are soft. Puree the mixture in a food mill, then press through a sieve. You should have about 2⅓ cups of puree.

Return puree to the pan. Over medium heat, stir in orange zest. Bring to a simmer, gradually stirring in the farina. Lower the heat and cook 2 to 3 minutes, until the mixture is translucent. Remove from the heat and cool for 5 minutes.

Stir, then pour into individual custard cups or wineglasses, or into a serving dish. Chill until set and ready to use. Serve very cold, topped with cream.

MASTER RECIPES

SWEET PASTRY

◆

You can use this delicate sweet crust with any of your favorite fresh fruit tart recipes.

ONE 9-INCH TART SHELL

- 1 **cup all-purpose flour**
- ⅓ **cup sugar**
  Pinch of salt
- 8 **tablespoons (1 stick) unsalted butter, cut into 1-inch pieces**
- 1 **large egg, lightly beaten**
- 1 **teaspoon vanilla extract**

Combine the flour, sugar, and salt in a medium bowl. Add the butter and cut in with a pastry blender or rub in with your fingers until the mixture resembles coarse crumbs. Stir in the egg and vanilla until well combined. (The dough will still be crumbly.) Pat the dough into the bottom of an ungreased 9-inch tart pan with a removable bottom. Refrigerate at least 1 hour.

Preheat the oven to 350° F. With a fork, prick the shell at ½-inch intervals over the bottom and sides. Bake for 15 to 20 minutes, or until pale golden. Cool on a wire rack before removing sides of pan.

EASY CREAM
CHEESE PASTRY

◆

The dough for this melt-in-your-mouth pastry is very easy to handle as long as it is first thoroughly chilled. The pastry is perfect for any fruit pie or fruit or jam-filled turnover.

ONE 8- OR 9-INCH DOUBLE PIE CRUST, ONE 10-INCH SINGLE PIE CRUST, SIX 8-INCH TRIANGULAR TURNOVERS, OR 12 TO 15 SMALL TARTS

1	cup (2 sticks) unsalted butter, at room temperature
8	ounces cream cheese, at room temperature
1	teaspoon vanilla extract
2 to 2⅓	cups all-purpose flour
¼ to ⅓	cup confectioners' sugar (optional)

Cream the butter, cream cheese, and vanilla in a mixing bowl. Gradually sift 2 cups of the flour into the bowl, mixing with a fork until the dough forms a ball. Add a little more flour if the dough is too sticky. Divide the dough in half. Wrap in plastic wrap and refrigerate 45 minutes or overnight.

Preheat oven to 425° F.

Lightly sprinkle a work surface with some of the remaining flour or confectioners' sugar. Flatten one dough ball into a thick disk. Lightly dust the dough and a rolling pin with a little flour or sugar. Using short, even strokes, roll the dough from the center into a circle 2 inches larger than the pie pan, turning the dough every few strokes and dusting it with flour or sugar as needed. Roll to about ⅛-inch thickness.

Lift the dough off the working surface with a pastry scraper and fold it in half and then into quarters to form a triangle. Place the pointed end of the triangle into the center of the pie pan and unfold so the dough drapes about ½ inch beyond the rim of the pan. (Or carefully roll the dough onto the rolling pin and transfer to the pie pan.) With your fingertips, firmly press the dough into the pan. Prick the bottom all over with a fork. Bake for 15 to 20 minutes, until just pale golden.

Freeze the remaining dough for another use. To make a double crusted pie, fill the shell. Roll the remaining dough to fit the top of the pie pan. Brush the rim of the shell with water and place the dough over the filling. Crimp with your fingers or press the tines of a fork dipped in flour into the dough around the rim to seal.

ALL-PURPOSE
FRUIT PIE CRUST

◆

There's no need for sugar in this crust since the fresh fruit fillings have their own sweetness. If you should like a sweeter crust, add 1½ tablespoons of sugar to the flour. Always roll the dough at least 2 inches larger than the pie pan.

ONE 9- OR 10-INCH DOUBLE OR TWO SINGLE PIE CRUSTS

3	cups all-purpose flour
½	teaspoon salt
1	cup (2 sticks) cold unsalted butter, cut into 1-inch pieces
1	tablespoon fresh lemon juice
4 to 8	tablespoons ice water

Put the flour and salt in a large bowl and mix well with a wooden spoon. Add the butter and cut in with a pastry blender or rub in with your fingers until the mixture resembles coarse crumbs.

With a large fork, stir in the lemon juice, then add the water one tablespoon at a time just until the dough is firm, moist, and pliable. Divide the dough in half. Roll into two balls. Wrap in wax paper and refrigerate at least 30 minutes.

On a lightly floured surface, flatten one ball of dough into a thick disk. Lightly dust the dough and a rolling pin with flour. Using short, even strokes, evenly roll the dough from the center into a 12- or 13-inch circle, about ⅛-inch thick, turning the dough every few strokes and dusting it with flour as needed.

Lift the dough from the surface with a pastry scraper. Fold it in half and then into quarters to form a triangle. Place the pointed end of the triangle into the center of the pie pan and unfold so the dough drapes about ½ inch beyond the rim of the pan. (Or carefully roll the dough onto the rolling pin and transfer to the pie pan.) With your fingertips, firmly press the dough into the pan. Fill as directed.

Roll the remaining ball of dough into a 12-inch round about ⅛-inch thick. Brush the rim of the shell with water and place the dough over the filling. Crimp the edges together with your fingers or press the tines of a fork dipped in flour into the dough around the rim to seal.

NOTE: The dough will keep for two days if put in the refrigerator, or tightly wrap and freeze for up to 1 month. Thaw before rolling.

CONNIE'S PIE CRUST

◆

This sweet crust is similar to a butter cookie.

ONE 8- OR 9-INCH LATTICE-TOP DOUBLE PIE CRUST

- **7 tablespoons confectioners' sugar**
- **1¾ cups self-rising flour**
- **8 tablespoons (1 stick) unsalted butter, cut into cubes**
- **1 large or extra-large egg, lightly beaten**

Mix the sugar with the flour in a medium bowl. Add the butter and cut in with a pastry blender or rub in with your fingers until the mixture resembles coarse crumbs. Bind the flour with just enough of the egg so the dough forms into a ball. Mix the remaining egg with a little water and set aside.

Dust the dough lightly with flour and place it between two sheets of plastic wrap. Using short, even strokes, evenly roll the dough from the center into a 10- or 11-inch circle about ⅛-inch thick, turning the dough every few strokes. Carefully remove the top piece of plastic wrap. Invert the crust onto the pie pan and remove the other piece of plastic wrap. With your fingertips, firmly press the dough into the pan. Trim to a ½-inch overhang. Reserve the scraps. Crimp the crust with your fingers or press the tines of a fork dipped in flour into the dough around the rim. Brush the bottom and sides of the dough with the remaining egg and water mixture. Refrigerate until ready to use.

To make the lattice, roll the reserved scraps into a flattened ball between 2 pieces of plastic wrap. Then roll ball into a 10-inch circle about ⅛-inch thick. Cut into ½-inch strips with a pastry cutter. Freeze or refrigerate in the plastic until ready to use.

To weave the lattice, moisten the rim of the bottom shell with water. Weave the pastry strips into a lattice over the filled pie shell. Evenly trim the strips and the edges of the pan. Seal by pinching the ends to the bottom crust.

CHEDDAR PASTRY

◆

For a sweet variation, cold apple juice can be substituted for the ice water.

6 DUMPLINGS

2½ cups all-purpose flour
 I teaspoon salt
 I tablespoon sugar
 ¾ cup vegetable shortening
 I cup (2 ounces) sharp Cheddar
   cheese, shredded, at room
   temperature
 ½ cup (8 tablespoons) ice water

Combine the flour, salt, and sugar in a bowl. Add the shortening and cut in with a pastry blender or rub in with your fingers until the mixture resembles coarse crumbs. Stir in the Cheddar. With a fork, stir in the ice water, one tablespoon at a time, until the mixture can be shaped into a ball. Wrap in plastic and refrigerate until ready to use.

Divide the pastry dough into 6 equal pieces. Roll out each piece between two pieces of wax paper to form a 7-inch square. Chill on a cookie sheet until ready to use.

CINNAMON SYRUP

This syrup and the Orange-Spice variation below both are good with any fresh fruit compote.

MAKES 1½ CUPS

1½	cups water
⅔	cup sugar
2	tablespoons unsalted butter
2	tablespoons maple syrup
1	teaspoon ground cinnamon

In a heavy saucepan, combine the ingredients and bring to a boil over medium-high heat, stirring until the sugar dissolves. Lower the heat and simmer 8 to 10 minutes, or until slightly thickened. Remove from the heat. Serve warm.

VARIATION

ORANGE-SPICE SYRUP. Replace ½ cup of the water with ½ cup orange juice. Omit the butter. Add 1 orange and 1 lemon, unpeeled and cut into quarters, 1½ tablespoons vanilla extract, 2 cinnamon sticks, 6 whole cloves, ¼ teaspoon whole allspice, ¼ teaspoon ground nutmeg, and ⅛ teaspoon allspice. Proceed as above. Strain the syrup before using. Serve warm.

CRÈME FRAÎCHE

◆

Why bother to buy this delicious topping when it's so easy to make? It is wonderful on any fruit dessert, served either straight from the jar or lightly whipped. It will keep about two weeks in the refrigerator.

MAKES 2 CUPS

½ **cup sour cream**
2 **cups heavy cream, preferably not ultrapasteurized, at room temperature**

Thin the sour cream with a little cream, then pour into the remaining cream. Pour the mixture into a clean glass jar, cover loosely, and let thicken at room temperature. This will take anywhere from 4 to 12 hours, depending on the warmth of the room. Cover the jar tightly and refrigerate. The crème fraîche will have the consistency of sour cream when thoroughly chilled.

VARIATION

◆

LIME CRÈME FRAÎCHE. Add 1½ teaspoons grated lime zest and 1 tablespoon lime juice to each cup of Crème Fraîche.

CRÈME ANGLAISE

◆

This is a standard custard sauce that can be poured over any fruit dessert of your choice. Substitute half-and-half or heavy cream for the milk if you prefer a thicker, richer sauce.

MAKES ABOUT 2½ CUPS

6 or 7	large egg yolks
½	cup sugar
2	cups low-fat or whole milk
2	teaspoons vanilla extract

Fill a bowl with ice cubes and cold water. Set aside.

Beat together the egg yolks and the sugar. Add the milk. Strain into the top of a double-boiler. Cook over simmering water, stirring constantly with a wooden spoon, until the sauce is thickened and coats the back of a metal spoon, about 15 to 20 minutes.

Immediately remove from the heat, continuing to stir. Plunge the pan in the bowl of ice water and stir until cool. Stir in vanilla. Strain sauce into a pitcher or bowl. Serve immediately or cover and refrigerate until ready to use.

HOT BUTTERSCOTCH SAUCE

◆

*M*ake this sauce just before serving and spoon over ice cream, cake, or your favorite dessert.

3 tablespoons unsalted butter
**1 cup firmly packed light brown
       sugar**
1/3 cup heavy cream

Combine the butter, brown sugar, and cream in a heavy saucepan over medium heat. Bring to a boil and cook, constantly stirring until the sugar is completely melted and syrupy. Remove from heat. As the hot sauce sits it will thicken.

ACKNOWLEDGMENTS

We'd like to give special thanks to the following people for their time, talent, and good appetites: American Spoon Foods, Pam Becker of General Mills, Inc., the California Strawberry Advisory Board, Leslie Cohen, Guiffara Bros Produce, Loree Goffigon, Bob Hecklau of the L.A. Nut House, Chris Kahn and the White Lily Foods Company, Barbara Lowenstein, Michael Maron, George Morrone, Terri Mouton of Frieda's Finest, Barry & Gust Nackos, the New Zealand Raspberry/Blueberry Board, Beverly Nickerson, Larry Nicola, Joe Patti, Peter Ritt of the Washington, Oregon, California Pear Board, Diane Rozas, Lauren Ryan of Dow Brands, Cathy Thomas, Steve Valentine, Marla Waltert, Shirley Wohl, and Sue Young.

INDEX

120